THE THEOLOGICAL METHOD OF JESUS

THE THEOLOGICAL METHOD OF JESUS

A COURSE OF LECTURES IN THE SUMMER
SCHOOL · HARVARD UNIVERSITY · 1905
By WILLIAM WALLACE FENN

BOSTON
THE BEACON PRESS, INC.
1938

COPYRIGHT, 1938, BY
THE BEACON PRESS, INC.

PRINTED IN THE UNITED STATES OF AMERICA

PREFACE

THESE lectures have been prepared for publication from manuscripts of a series of lectures, obviously written for oral delivery at the Summer School of Theology at Harvard University in 1905. Some allusions and some emphases betray the decade of their preparation. Nevertheless, the main argument is by no means outgrown, and seemed of sufficient moment today to be published even though the lectures could not receive that careful attention to each word and the general balance which those who knew Dean Fenn remember as so characteristic of his every published article and spoken address. I acknowledge here my grateful appreciation to PROFESSOR HENRY J. CADBURY of Harvard University for the work which he has done in reading the original manuscript and giving some very helpful general and technical advice.

DAN HUNTINGTON FENN

CONTENTS

LECTURE I.

THE CHARACTER AND SCOPE OF
OUR INQUIRY

IN the case of any notable man we are interested in methods as well as in results, asking first what he did and then how he did it. This is particularly true when one is dealing with a master in affairs of the mind. An historian, for instance, has certain material which he uses in certain ways; and in order to form a judgment as to his trustworthiness, we need to know both his sources and his method. It may be that he has had access to first-rate historical material which he has poorly used, in which case we neglect his conclusions and enucleate his valuable material, which is then worked up in a more accurate way. Or it may be that his method has been good, although the material at his command has been imperfect and unauthentic. In that case we respect and adopt his historical method, applying it to better and more complete material. When we have to do with one who is an originator of inspiring and directing ideas, it is especially essential to inquire into the origin and method of his thought. But it is even more essential when, as a religious leader, he touches the deepest springs of thought and feeling with the authority of a prophet from on high. The results are before us in Jesus' specific teachings, but our inquiry is as to the way in which he arrived at these results. We know what he thought, but the question is how he came to think as he did. And in such an investigation the term *method* should not be restricted to logical method alone, but may fairly be used to include materials also. Plainly, the purpose of such an inquiry is not merely to test the trustworthiness of his teaching, but also to extend and apply it, justly and in his spirit, to questions which he himself did not expressly consider.

It is, however, a somewhat novel undertaking to enter upon this inquiry in respect to Jesus: not that he is unworthy of it in point of interest and importance, for in truth, Jesus has proved himself the most influential person in all human history. No one has so deeply affected both directly and indirectly, the life of civilized man, because no one has touched so potently the sources of thought and conduct. And this influence gives no sign of abatement; on the contrary, it was perhaps never greater than now, and it bids fair to increase. Yet, although his teachings have enlisted the attention of scholars and won the hearts of men to a quite unequalled degree, the problem of his method —that is, how he came to think as he did—has scarcely been raised. Nor is this attributable to the opinion once expressed by Dr. Martineau in the earlier stage of his thought, to the effect that those are scarcely to be called Christian who, although concurring "with the views of Christ yet perceiving, as they imagine, how he came by them, regard him at best not as the Master of their faith, but as the fellow pupil with them of the same argument." Surely, to fall in with a teacher's method is far more convincing proof of discipleship than to adhere stoutly to his conclusions alone, without regard to his method. And, as we shall perceive incidentally in the progress of our study, the result is to establish the authority of Jesus, not according to the old but according to the new concept of authority upon an enduring foundation. No, a more plausible explanation is suggested by certain objections which may have been aroused by the mere announcement of our topic, brief examination of which will serve also to indicate more clearly the character and define more closely the scope of our inquiry.

First, it may be objected that Jesus was not a theologian at all and hence cannot have had a theological method. It is sometimes said that the distinction of Jesus lay in the fact that he was a man of pure religion and not at all a theologian in the sense, for instance, that Paul was. In view of the current deprecation of theology, this is often urged as a highly creditable distinction. Plainly, however, the discrimination rests upon a view of the nature of theology which is rapidly becoming obsolete. To speak bluntly, the present attempt to throw religion and theology into the divorce court is a device of the devil, which, besides being a grievous wrong to both parties, is working dire mischief in social and personal life. For what is theology but an interpretation and justification of religion in terms of thought, or to use Dr. Gordon's definition: "the just and inevitable expression in terms of the intellect of the life of the spirit." To separate religion from theology would mean that religion is not to affect the mind of man but is to remain a mere sentiment. Far be it from me to disparage the value of sentiment—but it needs no argument to prove that a sentiment which commands one's intellectual respect is worth more than an emotion which the mind ignores. The heart will not long love that which the intellect disdains or rejects. The affections will not permanently hold good that which the reason does not hold true. Wherever religion has sought to quarantine thought, humanity has calmly hoisted the yellow flag over the protected premises. Moreover, whoever thinks about religious experiences at all has and must have a theology—it may be true or false, good or bad, but a theology of some sort is inevitable for every man who really gives his mind to religion. Now Jesus unmistakably had thoughts about God and man and the relations which exist between God and man. These thoughts constituted his theology, even as his thoughts about the relation between men constituted his ethics. True, he was not a systematic theologian in the sense that he himself clearly formulated and articulated these ideas, in order to present them as a coherent and comprehensive system. Yet there was a real, if implicit, unity in his thought, as there is in the mind of every thoughtful preacher who gives little heed to the unity of his system as such. In the same way, a man of high and noble character seldom has a definite and formulated ethical system, although there is and must be a thought unity underlying his unity of conduct. With this unity of Jesus' thinking, however, we are not now concerned. Our endeavor is to discover the method of his thinking, taking for granted a sufficient knowledge of the main lines of his thought. The fact that he was a thinking man, who believed that God was to be loved with the mind as well as with the heart and who sought to communicate truth to men, constitutes him a theologian in the truest and most

[14]

just use of the term and warrants us in seeking for his theological method.

The second objection is more profound. It may be said that truth did not come to Jesus through intellectual processes, and therefore it is needless to seek for any method of thought. This objection may take either of two forms. On the one hand, it may be said that as a divine being, he knew truth directly, or, if you please, by unmediated revelation from God. On the other hand, it may be affirmed that as a religious genius he saw by insight, and was not dependent upon the cumbersome process of ratiocination. Clearly, the first form of the objection opens a problem too vast for our present consideration. It is, evidently, allied to a practically discarded theory of revelation, according to which God's truth has no relation to man's powers; only when the sun of reason sets does the light of God shine in upon the expectant soul. But we are now convinced, that, however and wherever truth may originate, when it appears in consciousness, it is and must be in the form of rational thought. But this objection should not prejudice our undertaking. If, upon investigation, we find that Jesus did have a plainly marked method of thought, of course, the *a priori* objection will be cancelled by the *a posteriori* fact. And, conversely, that fact will of necessity become a factor in determining our conception of the method of revelation, and the relation of Jesus to the word of God.

As to the second form of the objection, it will be conceded at once that Jesus was a genius, and that his thought was not attained by a conscious intellectual process. But if the insight of a genius be true insight, it does represent an

[15]

implicit intellectual process which the logician can make explicit. Good reasoning can be reduced to syllogistic forms, even though the reasoner himself never heard of "Barbara" or "Felapton." Perhaps Euripides could not have scanned one of his own choruses so well as a sophomore who has studied Schmidt, yet the form is there nevertheless. When we speak of the theological method of Jesus, therefore, it is not at all meant that he had a logical formula which he applied as, for instance, a young student of Hegel applies to all his problems the law of progress from undifferentiated unity through division into a higher unity. By no means does it follow that the method was consciously formulated or applied, but it may, nevertheless, have been real. To this form of the objection, therefore, as to the first, the ultimate answer must be an appeal to fact. Does a study of the teaching of Jesus reveal a method of thought which can be defended as valid and which we can, therefore, adopt in our theological thinking? Perhaps the discovery of such a method and its application would rescue theology from the imputation of unreality and make our religious thinking as vital and fruitful as the thought of Jesus himself.

LECTURE II.

A S a background for our study, it is necessary to speak briefly of the theological method of the contemporaries of Jesus to which we may for the sake of brevity refer as the scribal method. Let me repeat that we are to consider not merely the logical, but the theological method of Jesus. The larger title was deliberately chosen, because it includes both the logical method and the materials to which that logical method was applied. In considering the scribal method, therefore, we have to seek after both materials and logical forms. Speaking first, then, of materials, it is plain that on the whole the materials for scribal theology were derived from the Law, and in the last analysis from the Mosaic Law.

In saying anything about intellectual and social conditions contemporary with Jesus, we must guard against the error which has been so prevalent among Christian scholars—that of basing judgment upon a few data which are taken too seriously. Jewish scholars complain of us, and with obvious justice, that our whole representation of Judaism is vitiated by ignorance and misapprehension. Certainly, it is to be hoped that no Christian scholar will ever again write a life of Jesus in which contemporary Judaism will be represented as wholly given up to disputations about what kinds of knots might be tied on the Sabbath, or what burdens borne. It ought to be carefully remembered that many of the disputations to which Christian scholars have referred in disgust and scorn were purely academic discussions (as when a teacher of law supposes a case with all sorts of complications, designed to try the wits of his pupils) and did not so much as touch the actual life of the people. If, several centuries hence, some mousing antiquarian should try to reconstruct the nineteenth-century life of New England from arithmetics and books on etiquette, the result would be interesting but not especially accurate. He might say, for instance, that it was the custom for a man needing the service of a farrier to engage him to shoe his horse upon payment of a penny for the first nail, two pennies for the second nail, and so on in arithmetical or geometrical progression, until the last nail was driven. Conclusions might be deduced as to the fantastic erudition of blacksmiths and the simplicity of New England farmers, which would have little relation to conditions actually existing. Or, suppose that this antiquarian should come upon a book of etiquette or worse still, some unfortunately preserved correspondence columns of a monthly or weekly journal, in which anxious enquirers ask Penelope or some other ingenious person about social customs—what an impression he would form of the fierce conventionality of our life! The comparison is undoubtedly a little extreme, and yet there is substantial justice in saying that our popular impressions as to the contemporary life of Jesus are almost as grotesquely inaccurate.

With reference to the attitude of Judaism towards the Law for instance, if—neglecting chronology and giving certain passages their full face value—we were to form our judgment upon rabbinical quotations which describe

[18]

God as consulting the Torah when He would create the world and even now devoting the first three hours of each day to its study and proclaiming daily a new Halacha to the heavenly Sanhedrin, we should have a highly entertaining picture, but a gross caricature. A sense of humor is not entirely needless, even in an historical student. Yet, after making such needed allowances, it is just to say that the theological work of the Scribes was based upon materials derived from the Law, which was deemed of supreme authority because it emanated directly from God Himself. A theory held by some of the Rabbis, which ultimately prevailed against the saner view, was that since the Law in the stricter sense was given by God Himself, it was finally authoritative and thoroughly sufficient for all needs. Problems arising which were not explicitly provided for in the Law itself must be solved by implications carefully folded into its divinely chosen forms of expression. From this theory, thus broadly stated, two inferences were drawn among many others. First, that no single word or letter was to be treated as insignificant—"one jot or tittle could in no wise pass from the Law till all were fulfilled;" and second, that the authority of the Torah was to be carried over to the interpretations of its involved meanings. Hence, the Torah comes to mean not the books of Moses alone, but the whole Old Testament Scripture and even the unwritten traditional system of scribal interpretation, all of which is authoritative with the authority of the Torah whose explication it is.

It is not difficult to see how all this came about. It is the chief distinction of the Hebrew prophets that they had the courage to announce their highest ideals of duty as the word of the Lord, disobedience to which on the part of the people was disobedience to God Himself. In their hands, the relation between God and His people became ethically conditioned and teleological in character. In course of time, these two ideas were dissociated; the teleological idea appears in apocalyptic imaginings which have little or no ethical basis, and the ethical motive is debased into casuistry, with no breadth of view and no large, comprehensive outlook. It is this latter tendency with which we are most nearly concerned. The people were disobedient and the misfortune which befell Israel established the word of the prophet. When the Captivity ended, Israel emerged with a profound conviction that its future well-being depended solely upon obedience to the will of God. But what was His will upon fulfillment of which national prosperity was dependent? The simple, large teaching of the prophets was too indefinite—but was there not a precise code which had been given by the Lord unto Moses? So to this were attached the warnings and exhortations of the prophets, and thus the prophetic spirit was sacrificed. The prophets were honored by abandoning their spirit. It is an old story, often repeated in religious history: the influence of the prophet tends to tighten the yoke of bondage from which he has been emancipated and from which he sought to deliver others. And more precisely, this attitude of Israel towards the Law is entirely analogous to the attitude of Christendom toward the Scriptures and even toward its supreme Master, Jesus of Nazareth. When, for example, we read in the Talmud that there are two methods of interpreting Scripture—the Peshat or plain method according to which each passage is to be explained in the most natural way according to the letter, the grammatical construction, and the spirit of the passage; and the Derash, according to which artificial and recondite meanings are to be sought in the sacred text—we feel ourselves sadly at home. Nor are we surprised to find the elaborate driving out the plain interpretation, for precisely that has happened in the process of Christian interpretation; and the two forms of Midrash—the Halacha and Haggada—suggest irresistibly the theological and the homiletical use of the sacred text. That the authority of the Torah should have been carried over to the whole system of interpretations and applications is not inexplicable or exceptional. It is not inexplicable, for if the sense of Scripture is Scripture, the authority attaches, of course, to the interpretation. It is not exceptional, for often in Christian thinking divine authority has been claimed for a certain interpretation of a text, and for creedal systems supposed to be based upon the text. In truth, the Christian use of the Bible presents most striking and perfect analogy to the Jewish. The connection is not so much historical as psychological. It ill behooves us to speak disrespectfully of the Judaistic methods, since we ourselves have been under similar condemnation. Moreover, it was men enslaved by such theories who opposed Jesus in the flesh and have always opposed him in the processes of Christian history. But this may be left for individual reflection—my present point is that the materials of theological thought were derived by the Scribes at the time of Jesus, as often by Christian theologians since, largely, if not exclusively, from the Scripture.

Upon the logical methods of the Scribes we have not time here to enlarge. From what has been said we are prepared to find them hermeneutical in character. Hillel is said to have been the first to formulate rules of interpretation, which were probably for the most part codifications of principles already in vogue. Some two generations afterwards, Nahum of Gimzo added to these a method called extension and limitation. This method gave wholly illegitimate force to certain particles in the Hebrew text, which were regarded as divinely given signs that the passages in which they occur are to be enlarged or restricted in application and force. Rabbi Akiba in the next generation carried the same tendency forward. Although his contemporary Rabbi Ishmael set himself against this swiftly growing tendency by declaring that the divine Law speaks the ordinary language of men, he adopted the rules of Hillel, increasing their number from seven to thirteen. Moreover, although his rules were formally adopted, they are said not to have interfered with the use in actual practice of the method of Akiba. Thus we see, beginning with the time of Jesus himself, the growing tendency to the introduction of elaborate methods of dealing with the sacred text. These may fairly be termed logical methods of writing up the materials furnished by the Scripture. With such materials and by such methods, the theological work of the time was done.

LECTURE III.

NOW we must ask whether or not Jesus is in line with the scribal method and its materials and whether or not he uses them. Manifestly, the presumption is that he does not, since he had no training in the rabbinical schools. It is true that now and then we find teachings attributed to him which impress us as rabbinical in character. For instance, in arguing about the Davidic sonship of the Messiah, Jesus has recourse to a passage in the 110th Psalm in which David addresses the Messiah as his Lord. Jesus argues, if he calls the Messiah his Lord, how can he be his son? Or again, Jesus argues in behalf of immortality from the fact that in the place of the Bush, God says, "I am the God of Abraham, the God of Isaac, and the God of Jacob," contending that if these patriarchs had not then been living somewhere, God would have said "I *was* their God." There are a few passages like this in which Jesus seems to be using contemporary materials and methods. But when we come upon these passages in reading the Gospels, it affects us, to use Matthew Arnold's phrase, "like sand in the mouth." The arguments are no more convincing than Paul's argument for the relation between Jews and Christians, derived from the matrimonial infelicities of Abraham. We feel irresistibly and instinctively that here we have not the real Jesus. Shall we say that it is like David wearing the armor of Saul? At any

[23]

rate, he appears as a man arguing with methods not his own and in a fashion to which he is not accustomed.

A similar feeling of incongruity comes over us when we find Jesus affirming the validity of the Law, even to every jot and tittle. We are inclined, perhaps, to deem such passages mere interpolations; they are alien to the spirit of Jesus and contrary to his actual practice. It is sufficiently plain that he had little respect for the rabbinical traditions. They made the word of God of none effect. Hence, as in the case of the Corban practice, Jesus cites the commandment to honor father and mother against a practice supposed to be allowed by the Rabbis. But it is equally plain that his practice and teaching are adverse as well to the prescriptions of the Law. Not only with reference to divorce does he cite the Law against the Law, but in certain particulars he denies the Law itself. When, for example, in the controversy concerning clean and unclean meats, Jesus laid down a principle making clean all meats, was he not denying a distinction laid down in the Law itself, and denying it, not as in the case of divorce on the ground of another and earlier principle, but on his own authority? Must we say, therefore, that Jesus consciously and explicitly rejected the contemporary idea of the authoritative Law and that the passages referred to a moment ago are mere interpolations? This would probably be an erroneous conclusion, resting ultimately upon an idealized conception of Jesus, which can tolerate no inconsistencies in his thought. But why should we look for such absolute consistency in him, when we fail to find any absolute consistency even among his most thoughtful followers? Some who contend most zealously for the final and absolute authority of Jesus are advocates of war, resist evil with glorious vigor, and denounce indiscriminate charity, as if Jesus had never said "Resist not him that is evil," and "Give to every one that asketh of thee, and from him that would borrow of thee, turn not thou away." Nay, while the observance of the Lord's supper and the duty of Christian missions are strenuously and properly urged on the basis of the command of Jesus, little heed is paid to the injunction to wash one another's feet and to the promise about immunity from venomous reptiles and poison. In the face of such inconsistencies in the present Christian consciousness, and the palpable incongruities in our own thought of which we are not aware until some one calls our attention to them, is it surprising that we should find in Jesus inharmonious utterances concerning the Law? The truth probably is that Jesus, brought up, as we know, to revere the Scripture, nourishing his own deepest life upon the noble words of psalmist and prophet, kept his reverence throughout life and probably was not conscious that at various points his teaching was contradictory. The Scriptures had penetrated deeply into his soul. Their words came naturally to his mind in the supreme moments of his career; reminiscences of its language tinge his utterances. His speech is saturated with memories of psalm and prophecy. Still, he is independent without fully realizing how independent he really is. Bousset has briefly and pithily said that "the Scriptures spoke to him with an authoritative voice, but he heard only that to which his ear was attuned"—and so it is, indeed, with us. It is certainly not

[25]

true that the materials for his thought were derived, as in the case of his contemporaries, from the Scriptures exclusively or even largely. If we may at this point anticipate the subject matter of the next two lectures, it may be said that his thought rested ultimately upon his experience in the world of nature and of human life.

When he preached, it is said that the people marveled that he spoke with authority and not as the Scribes. Did not the Scribes speak with authority? Undoubtedly, but theirs was a derived, and his was a personal authority. His was the authority of personal experience, theirs was the authority of tradition. Indeed, it would not be unjust to say that the antithesis nowadays so common between the religion of authority and the religion of the spirit was never more manifest in Christian history than in the beginning of our era, when an unschooled man faced the representatives of an honored tradition, boldly proclaiming—"Ye have heard that it hath been said, but *I* say unto you," and appealed to the people who heard him with the severe words, "Why do ye not even of your own selves judge?"

As one reads the Gospels even casually, he is impressed by the emphasis which Jesus places upon the inner, personal life. Contemporary religious tendencies made external things of importance, but the look of Jesus was inward. He pleaded for a righteousness exceeding intensively, but not extensively, that of the Scribes and Pharisees. It was not greater scrupulosity, but deeper spirituality which he had in mind; not to hedge the Law about with external punctiliousness, but to put love, the spirit of the Law, in the heart. All about him men were trying to work

[26]

from the circumference to the center. The method of Jesus was exactly the reverse, to work from within outward. Make the tree good, and its fruit becomes good naturally and inevitably, but a spruce does not become an orange tree by hanging oranges on it. Men were interested in these things, so that they might come into right relations with God. But it was just because man is not dependent upon them for communion with God that Jesus protested against such externalism. Hence he introduces a new scale of values.

Was this the spirit of the ancient Law in the sense that all its enactments, positive and negative, are but various expressions of love? How could this be shown in the case of ritual laws—clean and unclean animals, for instance? But our interest is in the fact that Jesus thought so, and that to him nothing was of the Law which was not at once child and parent of love—proceeding from it and producing its larger meaning. Purity of heart and singleness of purpose were for him of utmost worth: for these alone man ought to be anxious, rather than for food and drink and raiment. Consequently, whatever does not affect this inner life is negligible. To eat food ceremonially unclean has no influence upon the heart, therefore it is of no importance religiously. To be pure within, cherishing no envious or lustful or unbrotherly thought, but living in love and good will for all men—this is essential in his eyes. Compared with this, all external forms and rites of religion are as nothing and less than nothing. This was principally because through such inner purity, as he knew by his own experience, man has communion with God. In an

[27]

essay upon *The Ethics of Christendom,* Dr. Martineau argued that the fundamental idea of Christianity is ascent through conscience into communion with God—and this, at all events, seems to have been the thought of Jesus. "Blessed are the pure in heart, for they shall see God"— thus he had come into communion with his Father, and not by the ways of the Scribes. The sanctity of the inner life, supremely significant because thus man finds the crowning blessing of God's loving presence, is fundamental in his teaching.

Now, out of such communion with God his words and deeds proceeded. But how were his thoughts born? This is, for our present purpose, all important. Was it through some unique revelation, or was it through means open to us all? Was it that new things were given him to see, in some celestial world, or was it that through this communion his eyes were opened to see deeper meanings in the ordinary circumstances and events of life? I venture to affirm the latter, notwithstanding the recent attempt to discover an ecstatic element in the character of Jesus. It is a most inviting theme, lying, however, slightly aside from the main path of our inquiry where, therefore, we must not pursue it. Although it is undoubtedly true that the "Greek Christ" has been overemphasized in theological portrayals, I want to say that the ecstatic Christ seems to me much farther from the truth. But, even if it be true that he had moments of rapture, there is no evidence that his thought was derived from them. He found God, not by closing his eyes to the world about him, but by looking at it more sharply and penetratingly.

[28]

To show this, we must study the form of his teaching with the presumption which seems quite natural and in need of no defense, that truth came to him in the way he taught it. In other words, he did not come by his thought in one way and then subsequently devise another way of presenting it. Truth appeared in his mind in the form in which he taught it. Now, as we consider the form of his teaching, we are instantly impressed by its homeliness. There is nothing weird or uncanny about it, nothing unwholesome or strange. When we read his words, we feel ourselves on the familiar ground of common life. There is nothing to indicate that the speaker was dwelling in a different world from ours. Here are the fields and flowers, the growing corn and the nesting birds, the ordinary processes of nature and habits of men. As there is nothing unearthly about his teaching, so there is nothing conventional about it. He is not using borrowed illustrations or customary forms of presentation—all of his teaching has the air of fresh and vivid personal insight, the mark of utter sincerity, in Carlyle's use of the word. If it be true, then, that Jesus learned as he taught, the suggestion would be that through his communion with God, his eyes were opened to divine meanings in common things. This is so significant for our purpose that it will profit us to look at the teachings of Jesus more closely from this point of view. We must keep this idea in mind, in order that we may see whether or not it is really true that the materials of his thought seem to have been derived from his experience with nature and with man.

[29]

LECTURE IV.

THEOLOGICAL MATERIALS: THE WORLD
OF NATURE

WE need only a glance into the Gospels to make it
evident that the teachings of Jesus are to an exceptional degree built up out of the natural life
which lay about him. In this respect, Jesus differs conspic-
uously from Paul who, doubtless because he was born in
Tarsus, "no mean city," and educated in Jerusalem, also a
city, shows almost no knowledge of country life. Paul drew
his illustrations from the sights of cities and the customs
of city folk. There is no evidence that he had an eye for
natural beauty. Neither had Calvin at Geneva, or such
New England theologians as Hopkins and Edwards. Occasionally, indeed, Paul ventures upon a figure derived from
husbandry, as in the case of the wild and the cultivated
olive in Romans II. But notwithstanding Ramsey's recent
attempt to prove that in this he is true to the habit of
grafting a wild olive branch into a cultivated tree, in order
to strengthen the latter, foresters know of no such practice
or of such possible effect, and we must still pronounce his
illustration inept. But where his knowledge is inaccurate,
and his use is infrequent, that of Jesus is precise and
abundant. The natural life of Galilee he knows well and
accurately. It enters into and permeates all his teaching,
evidently underlying his thought.

In this, too, Jesus differs from the Scribes, who also
taught in parables. In a most admirable little work entitled

Jesus, Wilhelm Bousset has said, "It is noteworthy that in the parables of the synagogue, almost nothing at all comes from nature and its processes. The rich and free manner of Jesus is shown most of all in that he, true son of the people, who had grown up remote from the rabbinical schools, lives and moves in nature with his parables."

When one has his eyes opened to this characteristic of Jesus' teaching, it is amazing to see how fully the contemporary life is depicted. The land is a land of vineyards, some of which, at least, are encircled with hedges and protected by a tower. Here and there in the fields there are open pits into which an animal, or perhaps even a son, might fall. There is also the fig tree to which Jesus more than once refers. He especially observed its tender branch at the opening of summer. The fig trees need cultivation, loosening of the earth about the roots and manuring for productivity. In the fields there are thorns among which the seed falls only to be choked, and from which men gather no profitable fruit. In the land there are the high mustard plant and the reed shaken by the wind, besides such garden herbs as mint and rue, anise and cumin. Flowers bloom in the fields, which to his eyes are more beautiful than Solomon in all his glory. Yet these, with tares and dry grass, are to be burned in the primitive house ovens. Over all are the impartial rain and sunshine. He knows the look of the sky portending rain and homely weather signs familiar to country folk. We see the lightning suddenly fling from one end of the heaven to the other, and the storm with its fierce gusts and down-pouring rain. So the earth and the sky are mirrored in the teaching of

[31]

Jesus. Wild animals are mentioned, like foxes, wolves, and such domestic animals as dogs, licking the sores of beggars who lie helpless at the rich man's gate, oxen, asses, goats, calves, kids, sheep, lambs, the camel, symbol of great size, and the gnat, type of minuteness, the birds of the heaven—the falling sparrow and the vultures gathering about their prey, doves and ravens, and barnyard fowl. But it is needless to continue the recital—for enough has been said to make plain the exceptional degree to which Jesus uses the natural life about him in his teaching.

Are we to suppose that this was a mere pedagogical expedient or, in other words, that Jesus used such means for the conveying of his thought alone? Did he reach his thought in other ways, and then clothe it in this garb, so that it might be the more easily understood? If this were the case, it would be in no way discreditable. It might, indeed, teach us preachers a useful lesson, for I doubt if our sermons smack of the natural world as the wayside talks of Jesus do. But I am inclined to believe that his use of the natural world is far more significant than this. "From the fig tree, learn its parable," he said to his disciples. Its parable, yes, from the fig tree and all the trees! Yes, all this marvelous natural world seems to have been in Jesus' eyes a parable of God! And the chief purpose in our study of the parables is to discover by their means how we may be enabled to read all the parables of nature. Could anything be more out of place than a study of the parables of Jesus which fails to open our eyes to the countless parables in field and forest and human life? A child does its example in the school arithmetic—not so

[32]

much for the sake of the specific problems, as that by this means he may learn how to do all similar problems. Perhaps never in all his life will he have to find out what it will cost to paper a room of the dimensions given in the book, and at the price per roll there set down. But he has learned how to do all similar problems by means of the specific problem. It is a pathetic commentary upon the method of teaching spelling, when *Sonny's* father in Ruth McEnery Stuart's story laments that, having learned how to spell phthisis from a blue covered speller in childhood, he had all his life been looking and longing for an opportunity to use the word in writing a letter, so that he might display his hard won knowledge. But similar folly seems to pervade most of the discussions of the parables which enter with minute detail into every part of the teaching. They never open the eyes of the student to see, as Jesus saw, the great parable of nature, from which he has given but a few specimens out of boundless wealth. The point is that Jesus had an eye for the parable of nature. He taught in parable, because truth came to him in parable. We know that in mature life it was his custom to withdraw from human companionship, so that he might spend the night in solitude on the hillside, or by the shore of the lake. The practice was undoubtedly a survival from boyhood. Of meditative turn of mind, he was wont to sit alone in the fields about Nazareth, and in those hours his great thoughts were born. One might cite him as proof of Wordsworth's lines:

[33]

One impulse from a vernal wood
May teach you more of man,
Of moral evil and of good,
Than all the sages can.

He had come to his thought not by poring over books, but by thoughtfully watching the processes of nature and the ways of man.

This will become plainer, if we look briefly at three of his parables of nature, showing how the observation of nature lies behind the thought which interprets his experiences. The religious life of his time was marked by scrupulosity and punctilious watchfulness. Doubtless, as was said in the second lecture, we are prone to exaggerate this. Still, there can be no question that the religious life was one of solicitude lest something should be done or left undone, which would inure to one's harm before God. A hedge was set about the Law to keep one from even getting near enough to it to break it. But to Jesus the religious life was preëminently natural, and we seem to find his thought in the parable of the seed growing secretly. "So is the Kingdom of God as if a man should cast seed upon the earth and should sleep and rise night and day, and the seed should spring up and grow, he knoweth not how. The earth beareth fruit of itself, first the blade, then the ear, then the full corn in the ear." "The earth beareth fruit of itself," there is an affinity between the seed and the soil, such that when the seed falls into the ground, it germinates and grows without the watchfulness of man. Disturbed by the fussiness attending the religious life which surrounded him, can we not imagine Jesus sitting alone in

the fields and watching the growing grain? There the seed
falls into the earth, and man goes about his work. But
meanwhile the seed grows. Are not the ways of God in the
hearts of men like His ways in the processes of nature? Is
there not affinity between the heart of man and the truth
of God, such that by implanting true principles, there will
be natural and automatic growth? Does not the growing
grain rebuke the anxious solicitude of man and teach a
truer way? At any rate, this was the method of Jesus—not
to enforce rules from without, but to implant principles
within, and trust the truth of God to the heart of man.
Especially noteworthy is the fact that Jesus allies the
Kingdom of God to the processes of nature. The grain
growing in the field teaches him of the ways of the Kingdom among men. And this conclusion holds, even if we
accept an interpretation of the parable looking in a quite
different direction, namely, that he is thinking primarily
that the arrival of the Kingdom can be neither hastened
nor hindered by human effort, but will come through supernatural agencies at the hour of God's appointment.
This does not seem to me quite so natural an interpretation of the parable as the one previously suggested. But if
it were true, it would be still more remarkable that Jesus
should have found in the regular course of nature the im-
agery with which to describe a supernatural coming of
the Kingdom.

Or again, as the mission of Jesus went on, and a little
group of followers gathered about him, certain among
them appeared unworthy, and it may be that others of his
disciples wished him to purge the company of its discred-

itable elements. But Jesus, who had seen weeds growing among the wheat in the fields of earth, knew how difficult it was in the early stages to discriminate between the tares and the wheat, and how impossible to root out the weeds from the midst of the wheat. True, a modern farmer, knowing that it is better to lose a season's crop of wheat than to let the tares mature and scatter the seed of future harvests, might willingly destroy both wheat and tares at once. But that was not present to the thought of Jesus. Men were prominent in his mind, not tares and wheat, and it will not do to destroy both good and bad. So the wheat field with its mingled tares and wheat taught him to let good and bad grow together until the time of the harvest. Was this why he let Judas remain in the company of the disciples? Or was it a protest against the separatism of the Pharisees? "The field is the world," may suggest his answer to the deeper problem raised by the presence of evil in the world of God. Perhaps we can never be certain which view was foremost in the mind of Jesus. It is evident, however, that he was more interested in preserving the good than in eradicating the evil and was willing to leave the judgment to time and to God. There are evil men and good men in the world—yes, as in the fields of earth there are wheat and tares. But since they grow together in the field, let them also grow together in the world until the time of the harvest. That is God's way with men and man's way with the fields. Again, Jesus finds the answer to his problem in the world of nature.

Let us take but one more illustration. As Jesus preached and crowds gathered around him, there seemed to be an enthusiastic reception of his words. But Jesus was not deceived. Was not the fate of his words among men that of seed cast upon the ground? Hence he speaks the parable of the sower, as we rather inappropriately call it, for it is in reality the parable of the soils. In the parable, six kinds of soil are described. There is the trodden ground on whose hard surface the seed falls only to be caught up by watchful birds. There is the thin soil where the ledge comes near the surface in which the seed quickly germinates and then, because of the heat and the lack of nourishment, as speedily withers away. There is the thorny ground where the seed sprouts but is soon choked by the thorns. Such is the fate of seed, cast into the ground, and is not the fate of the word very similar? Some are instantly caught away, some quickly germinate, but as quickly wither, some grow a little more but are crowded out by thorns. There are listeners who give quick emotional response. They are ready to follow their Master whithersoever he may go, they are profuse in cries of "Lord, Lord," but they have no root in themselves and their emotional fervor speedily passes away. There are men, like the Pharisees, whose hearts are hard—"gospel hardened" in the fine New England phrase—and upon whom his words can produce no effect. Both of these, also, he had seen among those clustering around him as he taught. There were also men who seemed to make response. But their lives were so full of other things, so engrossed with the cares and anxieties of life, that the word never came to fruitage. Then there was the good ground—all good but with degrees of fertility, some thirty, some sixty, some an hundred fold, and so was it also among men. The six kinds of soil, the six kinds of hearers. Why should he be surprised at the varying treatment accorded his words, when there was similar diversity in the soil of a farmer's field? Thus the natural world again solves the problem of Jesus, and out of that world his thought is derived. The sower casts his seed broadcast, not trying sedulously to choose his soil. This is the way in which Jesus teaches.

But the progress is slow—yes, Jesus does not anticipate quick returns. How could he, having once laid hold upon the idea that the ways of God in the soul of man are analogous to the ways of God in the processes of nature? There is growth, the blade, the ear, the full corn in the ear. There is vast increase from small beginnings to large issues. Yes, this mustard plant, big as it now is, was once a tiny seed, the smallest, Jesus thought, of all seeds. Yet to this it has grown. "Who hath despised the day of small things!" Confident that he was speaking God's truth, confident that human hearts were congenial to the truth and that the forces of growth were co-operative and sure, he was not disturbed by present small results. Again nature answered his question and cheered his faith.

This is characteristic not of Jesus' parables alone, but also of his more didactic teaching. The grass of the field which God surpassingly clothes with beauty, and the birds of the air which he sufficiently feeds, speak to him of an even more watchful care over more precious man. That the sunshine is spread and the gentle rain falls over fields of saint and sinner alike is evidence to him of a love of God which stays not at the utmost bound of human iniquity.

As there are signs in the heavens of approaching storm, so there are signs of the times which the eye of spiritual perception has power to read. Instances of this sort, drawn from parable and precept, might be multiplied indefinitely. But surely enough has been already said to justify the assertion that the materials of the thought of Jesus were derived, in part at least, from his experience in the world of nature. His thought was one with the blowing clover and the falling rain, because through these and through all the processes of nature God was teaching him of His truth. It is not for us, at present, to consider whether or not this method was justifiable. Neither shall we consider whether or not, if adopted, it warrants the conclusions which he drew. That will engage our attention hereafter. Let us at least understand now, however, that his thought is that of one who lives largely out of doors and does his thinking there. His distinctive thought does not come from the schools nor from much study of authoritative written documents, but in part, at least, from his intercourse with nature, which he studies with attentive eye. "He that hath eyes to see, let him see; he that hath ears to hear, let him hear." The great parable outspread before his eyes is unrolled before all eyes. From the rising of the sun unto the going down of the same, God speaks to the world. "Day unto day uttereth speech, night unto night showeth knowledge." The invisible things of God from the foundation of the world are clearly seen. They are distinguished from the things that are made. Paul understood this theoretically, but Jesus knew it practically and learned to read the lesson of nature's wondrous parable. How much wider and deeper than his is our knowledge of nature! Shall we not also, taught by him, learn to read its parables?

LECTURE V.

HOW early in his career the priest's son, whom we know as John the Baptist, revolted from the priestly conception of religion, quite in the spirit of Micah the prophet, and withdrew into the wilderness, that there he might nourish a different type of piety, we have no means of determining. It is written, however, that he "was in the deserts until the day of his showing unto Israel." But of his far greater disciple, perhaps also a kinsman, who afterwards revolted from the scribal way of life, as he did from the priestly, it is written, after the scene when he was found as a boy in the temple among the doctors both hearing and asking them questions, that he went down with his parents to Nazareth and was subject unto them. John in the wilderness, Jesus leading the ordinary life of men as a carpenter in Nazareth, this difference between the two appears in their public careers and in their religious teaching. "John comes neither eating nor drinking," Jesus is found at wedding-feasts, and of him it was said—"Behold a gluttonous man and a wine-bibber." The disciples of John fasted, while the followers of Jesus were as men at a wedding-feast for gladness of heart. Hence it is not surprising that John figures as a stern censor of contemporary life, condemning it, as it were, from the outside, while Jesus appears, to use Zangwill's pregnant if somewhat extravagant term, "As a joyous comrade, seeking to uplift and guide the life of his fellows from within."

[41]

Whether or not it was so at first we cannot tell, but certainly from the time of his public appearance, we find him associating with the ordinary folk, especially with those who in the eyes of strict religionists, were deemed profane and accursed because they knew not the Law. Perhaps the scene in the temple indicates an early interest on the part of Jesus in the Scribes and their teaching. It is undoubtedly true that in certain respects Jesus had come under scribal influence. Although eminently of the prophetic order, he teaches like a Scribe. He was the teacher with his disciples, rather than the prophet with awed listeners. And his *method* of teaching also was that of the Scribes. They also employed parables and pithy epigrammatic sayings for the communication of their thought. Indeed, to many of his parables there are close parallels in the Rabbinical writings, which, since we can hardly suppose that he borrowed them, must indicate either that both were drawing from a common stock or that his stories were suggested by theirs. The fact that he was a teacher— indeed popularly called Rabbi—and that he taught in parables, allies him with the Scribes and at least suggests some familiarity with their methods. However, there can be no doubt that, during the significant period of his career, his intercourse was not with them, but with the common people. He was one of them by birth and bringing up, and in them he found humanity in the grain. Sham, pretence, mere conventionality were odious to him, and in these simple folk he found sincerity, responsiveness, which appealed to him and drew him and them together. In the manuscript (Codex Bezal) there is an interesting addition which relates that once Jesus saw a man working on the Sabbath and said, "If thou knowest what thou art doing, thou art blessed; if thou knowest not, thou art accursed." It is a highly significant saying. Both he and those with whom he associated were alike in their freedom from anything like religious scrupulosity. But in his case it was the result of principle, while in theirs it may have been due to carelessness, indifference, or perhaps to actual sin. But naturally they came together—and the Scribes must have deemed both him and them guilty of heinous and dangerous laxity.

Hence it is as Wernle has said with great point, that the religion of Jesus is a layman's religion, because its prophet and founder from the point of view of the priests on the one hand, and the Scribes on the other, was a layman. Now, as his parables from human life show, it was in this free and confiding intercourse with men that truth came to him. They also show that he was far more familiar with men in the lowly walks of life, engaged in their customary occupations, than with those of higher station. Hence parables relating to this sphere of life have far more verisimilitude than those which attempt to describe the life of wealth and outward circumstance.

Not only in the ways of nature, but also in the ways of ordinary human life, then, Jesus sought and found the revelations of God. The shepherd, pursuing after that which was lost and searching until he finds it, speaks to him of the tireless quest of God. Similarly, the shepherd guiding and feeding his flock tells of the guidance and protection of God for his people. The cultivator, digging about the roots of an unfruitful tree and manuring it in hopes that it will yet bring forth fruit to justify its place in the garden which it now uselessly drains, is in Jesus' eyes a symbol of God offering to an unfruitful people one last chance of proving itself worthy of his care. The master of a vineyard, giving to the last even as to the first, tells of the Father's grace. The owner of a vineyard, sending for its products and finding his messengers treated with contempt and bodily harm, suggests the messages of God to rebellious Israel. Thus the few and simple occupations of the humble folk whom Jesus knew impart to him lessons of religious significance. Fishermen sorting their catch on the shore, a sower casting seed upon the earth, a housewife mixing a batch of dough, a merchantman seeking goodly pearls—all these matters of daily observation and experience tell the secrets of the Kingdom of God, and from them he draws his thought and his teaching. While he is thus in the way of reason, truth takes form in his mind, not while he is in ecstatic raptures.

So thoroughly is Jesus dependent upon his personal experience that when, as occasionally happens, he speaks a parable relating to walks of life with which he was unfamiliar we feel the difference at once and recognize the comparative infelicity of the story. When, for instance, we hear of a rich master's dealing with a retinue of servants or with upper servants to whom he entrusts large property, the parable is vague and lacks verisimilitude. He speaks of talents committed by a wealthy owner to his servants much as a countryman today speaks of a million—merely as a conventional term for the largest sum of which he has any conception. But his references to the conduct of inferior servants in the house toward those in even more subordinate place, or to the treatment accorded a servant by a master who can afford but one, are singularly vivid and realistic. There is a parable, for example, of a master with but one servant who, after toiling in the field all day, must prepare and serve his master's meal at night. The very fact that a man is well enough off to have one servant and too poor to have more than one would make him, as every student of human nature is aware, exacting and ungracious—does he thank that servant because he did the things that were commanded him? Similarly, the harshness of subordinates to their inferiors is often mentioned. The servant whom the master has left in charge during his absence begins to beat his fellow-servants and to live riotously. The servant who has himself been forgiven a great deal goes out and finds his fellow-servant, who owes him but a trifling sum and seizes him by the throat, gruffly crying—"Pay me that thou owest." When the latter begs for an extension of time, promising full payment almost in the very words in which the former had just pleaded for mercy, and obtained it, he meanly refuses and proceeds to the last extremity. Jesus knew well the cruelty of weakness and inferiority invested with temporary power and makes large use of it in his parables.

It is with this in mind that we must understand certain of the most difficult and troublesome parables of Jesus. Let me illustrate by reference to two of the most vexing parables, that of the Unjust Steward, and The Laborers in the Vineyard. In the case of the Unjust Steward, we feel at once that in the dealings of the master with his servant, Jesus is on unfamiliar ground. It is quite impossible to form a clear picture of the dishonest steward's transactions in wheat and oil. "How much owest thou my lord?" And he said, "A hundred measures of wheat." And he said, "Take thy bond and sit down quickly and write fifty," and so on with the other debts which he similarly scales down. Is it possible to represent this commercial transaction by any methods conceivable either then or now? Would a master, sufficiently convinced of the dishonesty of his servant to discharge him, have permitted him to remain in a position where such further knavery would be within his power? Is it within the bounds of possibility that, having detected the swindle, he would have commended the unjust steward? Is it not apparent that in attempting to describe business transactions, Jesus is off his own ground and is in no better case than a modern clergyman who should undertake to describe transactions on the Board of Trade, of which he has only vague knowledge? And yet, the point of the parable is in a phase of life with which Jesus was well acquainted, and of which he had intimate knowledge. The steward, soon to be out of a position, feeling too feeble to work and too proud to beg, is at his wit's end to know what is to become of him. And what is his device— is it not to trust himself to the gratitude of the simple folk who are his lord's debtors? He scales down their obligations, thus winning their gratitude, in order that when he is cast out by his master, they may receive him into their homes. Truly, a shrewd scheme, and Jesus knew well that he could thus safely trust to the gratitude of men and women of the sort with whom he was dealing and whom Jesus knew so intimately. This is the lesson of the parable —the worth of gratitude, of friendliness, making friends out of your money instead of making money out of your friends—that when ye fail ye may be received into the everlasting habitations. The man of this world who knows enough to put his trust in grateful, friendly hearts is wiser than the children of light ignorant of this. Now, this is a sound principle—every shop-keeper knows that it is better to lose a little on a trade than to stand stoutly for his rights and forfeit the good will of a customer. But the significance of the parable for our purposes is that it illustrates the way in which the personal knowledge and experience of Jesus enters into his teaching. We see that the value of the teaching is enhanced when it is derived not from conventional knowledge, but from his own personal observation in ways of life which he intimately knew.

A similar lesson is taught by the story of the laborers in the vineyard. With the sociology of the parable we are not particularly concerned. Doubtless, it was an entirely unbusinesslike proceeding. There was some reason for complaint on the part of those who, having toiled all day under the blazing sun, received at the day's close only the regular wage, which was given also to those who had worked but a single hour. To be sure, they got the stipulated wage. But we cannot help feeling a little sympathy with their sense of injustice and wrong. We wonder, also, how this master of the vineyard would have fared the next day, when he went out to seek laborers for his vineyard. Perhaps he would have found very few in the market place at the early hours, but many at the eleventh hour. They might have reasoned that, in view of the yesterday's transaction, it would be the height of folly to work more than the one hour, if for that a day's pay was given. Thus, in fact, men have reasoned in the higher realms toward which the parable points. And the eleventh hour has inspired many a man to have his fling in youth and manhood, bringing to God at last only the fag ends of his life and expecting thus to get the full of both worlds. Surely, there are very infelicitous elements in the parable, and not even Ruskin can fully satisfy us as to the economic truth of it. Yet Jesus was not speaking as an economist. Neither—and here is the point of the parable—was he considering the matter from the point of view of the employer, but solely from the point of view of the man out of work. Here were men entirely dependent upon their daily labor. It is a commodity which cannot be stored. Today's labor must be sold today, or its gain is lost beyond recovery. So these men go eagerly into the market place in the morning and wait for employment. But no man hires them, and the anxious hours pass, carrying with them their hope and courage. They stay in the market place, hoping against hope, not quitting it even when the shadows grow long and the chance of work is practically gone. At the eleventh hour work comes, and they go into the vineyard. It is not said that they worked any more zealously than their companions who had labored all the day. It is by no means intimated that they had earned the wage they received. The simple teaching is that they received a full day's pay for a twelfth of a day's work. Jesus is looking at the matter from the point of view of these men out of work, lingering despairingly about the market place. Their lot has been harder, because of its discouragement and despair that day than the lot of those who have toiled in the vineyard. Jesus knows this. Thus, again, his sympathy with the poorer folk with whom his lot in life was cast appears in his teaching.

This may, perhaps, appear in another way worth suggesting, at least because of the vista of thought it opens. A recent writer in the *Spectator* has said that one notable fact in the teaching of Jesus is that it seems strikingly deficient in the sense of justice. There is much more to be said for this idea than the writer in the *Spectator* has said. Do we not vaguely feel this in reading some of the parables? There is a man who accidentally comes upon a treasure hid in a field. Carefully covering up his find, he scrapes together money enough to buy the field and secure the treasure. But is this conduct just? When in our time, for instance, a bibliophile finds in the possession of a family ignorant of its value, a first edition which is an almost priceless treasure and buys it for a song—is the act ethically admissible? What about the justice in the conduct of the man who finds a treasure hid in the field? Jesus never considers that question at all. He knows the satisfaction of the finder and never thinks of the justice of the transaction. Or again, in the parable of the servant forgiven the great debt, we find the lenient creditor requiring the payment of the debt he had once canceled, casting his debtor into prison and commanding his wife and chil-

[49]

dren to be sold. What about the justice of demanding payment of a debt once forgiven? Doubtless, like Jesus and the other servants, we rejoice to see the cruel servant get his "come-up-ance," but again what of the equity of the transaction? Could an ethical or religious teacher nowadays tell the story of the servants who traded with their lord's money, winning large increase, without raising the question of the way in which the money was used and how the gain was acquired? Did it represent the gain of oppression? Was it the result of trading upon the necessities of others? Certainly no one, whose conscience is offended that the light to lighten the Gentiles is fed with Standard Oil, could help raising these questions. Such instances as these, like the parables of the unjust steward and the laborers in the vineyard just considered, lead us to wonder whether or not it is really true that our stern Teutonic sense of justice had actually less place in the mind of Jesus than the virtues of benevolence, pity, and charity. It is true that on account of the conditions in which the lot of Israel was cast during and after the exile, justice came to mean giving the oppressed his rights, showing mercy to the down-trodden and the poor, rather than distributing even-handed justice. It may well be that this had so left its effect upon the thought of Jesus, that from the poverty of his life he laid stress upon pity, mercy, charity, rather than upon justice as we conceive it. This, however, is thrown out as a mere suggestion. If acceptance of it should somewhat strengthen the idea that Jesus derived his thought from the experience of the common folk, rejection of it would not impair the idea sufficiently established on other grounds. The point to be insisted upon is that the thought of Jesus shows its origin in his experience with the ways of common life, as well as in the ways of nature. This will become perfectly plain if we consider together the greatest and best of all the parables of Jesus—that of the Prodigal Son—in which, dealing with domestic life, Jesus is plainly on familiar ground and at his best.

The more one studies this parable, the more is he impressed by what may, without offence, be called its marvelously artistic character. What did Jesus see in those whom others deemed the outcasts of society which drew him to them? He has answered our question in the story of the Prodigal Son by a succession of most exquisitely beautiful touches. He has told it in such a way that as we finish the parable, our love for the prodigal in the story is as strong as his, for he has revealed to us the nobility of the wayward son. What does the parable tell us of the home from which the prodigal wandered? The father was, plainly, a man of a type by no means unfamiliar among us—austere and hard to outward appearance but with a great tenderness at heart, of which his children never became aware. If the younger son had really understood his father, he never could have dreamed of going back to become a servant in the household: he knew that the poorest servants were well fed and cared for, and he wanted to have place with them. But it never occurred to him that his father's love was too great to permit such treatment of a son. The revelation of paternal affection on his return was a great surprise. He had never before known his father to disclose the wealth of loving feeling underneath his austere exterior. Of the two sons, the one seems to have inherited the father's real, the other his apparent nature, for the elder brother is in reality what the father only seemed. Not only does he refuse a welcome to the returned prodigal—the father's "thy brother" is in gentle rebuke of his contemptuous "thy son"—but he puts the worst construction upon his brother's conduct. The word translated "riotous living" means simply: living as a spendthrift. Although he probably led a wild and sinful life, that which may be implicit in Jesus' description of it is made brutally explicit in the elder brother's expression "devoured thy living with harlots." But that was the elder brother—respectable, dutiful, hardworking, but hard and bitter and cruel. All these years, "I slaved for thee neither transgressed I at any time thy commandments." Did the Pharisees recognize themselves in the picture? In such a home so delicately intimated, the future prodigal grew up, ardent, fond of pleasure, emotional, yet with nothing in his home life to satisfy the legitimate longings of his nature. Wondrously significant is the protest of the elder brother, "Thou never gavest me a kid that I might make merry with my friends," and his surprise at the quite unwonted light and music of the home when he came back from the field, where he had been industriously at work. Significant, for Jesus would have us understand that there had been in the past little or no merrymaking in the austere household. Is it surprising that from such a home, with a father grievously misunderstood largely by his own fault, and with a brother only too well understood, the younger son was eager to be gone? Thus with the thought-

[52]

lessness of youth he asks for a division of the property in anticipation of his father's death and goes into a far country—a Jewish youth into the land of aliens. There he lives like a spendthrift until his patrimony is squandered. When he has spent all and the famine comes, he finds himself in want. Again, by a succession of most delicate touches Jesus makes us feel the real nobility of the youth, as it gradually appears in his time of need. His first thought is to find work. He will not live by his wits, he will work. He is not squeamish about his job. He goes and joins himself to a citizen of that country, and he sent him into his fields to feed swine—fine work for a Jew of wealth! From this point on, those of us who have had experience with men who have quoted to us the parable of the prodigal begin to realize the innate worth of this boy in the story, for the last thing that the modern prodigal wants is work, especially such degrading work. Often when I have suggested to a young man, who has pitifully called himself a prodigal, this aspect of the parable and advised him to go and do likewise, to work on the streets until something better turned up, I have been met with reproaches, and at least once with curses, which showed that my visitor was not at one with my exegesis of the parable. Work, any work, however mean—the fact that this was the prodigal's real desire gives us the first touch of the genuine worth of the boy. But the work is insufficient, and his hunger increases. He "comes to himself" and makes two manly resolves. The first is to go home and take service with his father. What a blow to his pride! Back to the home which he had left only a short time before in pride and prosperity, back to meet the hardness of the father and the contempt of his brother, perhaps the scorn of fellow servants and the derision of neighbors who had watched his departure—back in wretchedness and want. It took the spirit of a man to make such a resolve. How many modern prodigals have said to you when you advised them to return to their comfortable home, "Not in this condition! When I can get on my feet again and go back in a decent way, I will. But I am too proud to return like this!" The prodigal in the story, however, was above this foolish pride and with genuine manliness turns his face homeward. He accepts the responsibility for his condition, "I have sinned," not, "I have been unfortunate." There is no attempt to concoct a pathetic hard-luck story. On the contrary, there is a frank, manly acceptance of responsibility for his own condition and a sincere confession of unworthiness. There is hope for a man who is down, when he is willing to confess his own fault and call his sin by its right name. The sincerity of his nature appears splendidly when, received by his father with a kindness he had no reason to expect, he nevertheless says that which in the far country he had determined to say. Instead of trying to work upon his father's sympathies still more, he confesses his sin and unworthiness. Yet with all the mercy and forgiveness shown in this parable, Jesus gives no countenance to any loose or weak view of sin. When the father says to the elder brother, "All that I have is thine," we realize that, notwithstanding the prodigal's return and the newly discovered love of his father in which he rejoices, he has lost something by his sin and folly which cannot be restored.

[54]

He has had his share of his father's goods and wasted it, he has had his chance and lost it. Some things lost are lost forever, and his sin has consequences which restoration to his father's love cannot avert. Thus the parable ends, leaving us with a feeling toward the prodigal which enables us to understand the love which Jesus had for those who were deemed the outcasts of society.

I have dwelt upon this parable at such length because it appears to me to show, better than any hurried references to many parables could, the deep familiarity of Jesus with the ways of men, out of which his thought was born. Whence came the materials of his thought, where did he look for revelations of God? Not to Scriptures, sacred as they were, but to the ways of nature and the ways of men, where lessons were taught him which he taught to men with a personal and not a derived authority. Having said so much about the materials of Jesus' thinking, let us leave the last suggestion on this point for a time and pass now to a consideration of the logical method applied to these materials, by which he rose from ordinary human experience to the ways of God.

LECTURE VI.

THE THEOLOGICAL METHOD OF JESUS

IT will serve to make more explicit, perhaps, the idea we have been considering, if we can see how the thought of Jesus which proceeded, as has been said, out of his experience in the ways of nature and the paths of men developed with accumulating experiences. Obviously, this is an exceedingly difficult undertaking. Our Gospels are not the work of trained historians, interested as historians now are in tracing processes. Indeed, it has sometimes been said that there is no indication of any modification in the thought of Jesus from the beginning to the end of his ministry. In two very important particulars, however, it seems to me possible to trace such development, namely, in his attitude toward the Messiahship and toward the world outside of Israel. And I speak of these in particular, because the latter point has been raised in private conversation during the course of these lectures and because the first is the very storm-center of present New Testament discussion. It also has important bearing upon Jesus' idea of the Kingdom of God, to which I must refer briefly at the close of the present lecture.

I. Jesus and the Idea of the Messiahship.[1]

It has become generally recognized that the scene at Caesarea Philippi marks a definite crisis in the life of

---

[1] The lecturer was fully conscious of the difficulties involved in the position which is here developed. When he was confronted with the choice between preserving the interpretation of the text and the moral integrity of Jesus, he chose to save the latter. *Ed.*

Jesus. Holtzmann's arrangement of the successive crises has much to commend it. In his opinion the discussion concerning clean and unclean meats, which is followed by the significant words—"From thence he arose and went away into the borders of Tyre and Sidon" (Mark 7:24) marks a decisive break with the religious leaders of Jesus' own people. Their attitude toward him became so threatening after the plain-spoken repudiation of a practice for which martyrs had died in the Maccabean Age and which was plainly taught in the sacred Scriptures, that he turned away from his own people into the parts of Tyre and Sidon. Presently, however, we find him back again in the vicinity of the Sea of Galilee, but, significantly, on the east side of the Jordan, for the most part in Decapolis and Bethsaida, with apparently but one brief visit to the western shore. There he has another encounter with the Pharisees, and thence promptly returns again to the eastern side, where we find him at Caesarea Philippi, far to the north. It seems as if Jesus were about to abandon Galilee for reasons of safety and devote himself to regions beyond Herod's jurisdiction, out of the sphere of influence of his bitterest opponents. But after the scene at Caesarea Philippi, we find him back in Galilee again, and at Capernaum, although with some slight show of secrecy. Then he is on his way to Jerusalem, the very center of danger, evidently with a premonition of certain calamity and death. What had happened at Caesarea Philippi to effect this change? Plainly, the declaration to his disciples in response to Peter's impetuous confession that he was actually the Messiah. It is as the avowed Messiah that he goes to Jerusalem, solemnly warning his disciples both at Caesarea Philippi and on the way, that he is going to his death. If we can trust the report which represents Jesus as saying to Peter, on the latter's declaration of his Messiahship—"Flesh and blood hath not revealed it unto thee, but my Father who is in heaven," the conclusion is unavoidable that up to this moment, Jesus had never avowed himself the Christ, even to his disciples, much less to others. This conclusion seems to be winning large acceptance among New Testament scholars, but a further inquiry instantly arises. Had Jesus known himself as the Messiah prior to this event, when he declared himself such to his disciples? Apparently such scholars are inclined to hold that the scene at the baptism marks his clear consciousness of the Messianic vocation, which he kept to himself until the opportune moment should arrive for declaring himself the Messiah. This came at Caesarea Philippi for the disciples, and on Palm Sunday for the multitude. Still, a study of the scene at the baptism leaves one uncertain whether or not the vision and the voice reported require or will even bear this interpretation. It is quite as likely that he then became fully conscious of divine sonship, for the words "My beloved son" certainly carry no necessary implication of Messiahship, and at most would involve in the circumstances only the conviction of a special call to divinely appointed service, which may perfectly well have been the beginning of his prophetic mission. It appears evident that a period of temptation followed the baptism. But the detailed story of the temptation which appears in Mark and Luke seems from in-

THE THEOLOGICAL METHOD OF JESUS

ternal evidence to be a parable of Jesus, spoken much
later in his career, and inserted here because of the inti-
mation in Mark that there was a temptation following the
baptism. One would hesitate to place the dawning of his
Messianic consciousness here at the baptism, unless there
were evidence that from this time on he declared himself
the Messiah. But what evidence is there for this? Indeed,
what evidence can there be if, as it was alleged, Jesus,
knowing himself the Messiah, kept the secret close from
the time of the baptism until Caesarea Philippi? But is
there evidence to the contrary? When Jesus begins to
preach, it is with the words of John upon his lips—"The
time is fulfilled and the Kingdom of God is at hand: re-
pent ye and believe in the Gospel" (Mark 1:15). The
Kingdom is at hand, but does not the coming of the
Kingdom synchronize with the coming of the King? If
the Kingdom is only at hand, is the King actually present? Moreover, in a most curious passage in Matthew
10:23, we find Jesus sending out the Twelve to preach
but forbidding them to preach to the Gentiles or Samaritans. He says—"Ye shall not have gone over the
cities of Israel, till the Son of Man be come." If the
term "Son of Man" has here definite Messianic con-
tent, the coming of the Messiah was still in the future
and was presumably another than Jesus himself. We
cannot carry the words forward to the end of his life,
making them refer to a second coming. For at that stage
of his career his thought reached beyond Israel to the
outside world, and he cannot thus have restricted the
mission of the Twelve. Nor can we deem the word unau-

[59]

thentic, for there would obviously be no reason for inventing such a saying to put on the lips of Jesus, especially since the tendency manifest was to represent Jesus as possessed throughout his whole public ministry with an assurance of his Messiahship publicly avowed. The Caesarea Philippi incident enables us to deal critically with this tendency in the Gospels prior to that event. May it not be that this highly significant passage enables us to affirm that at this period of his ministry Jesus, like John, was looking for a Messiah—whom he does not yet believe himself to be?

It is at least a plausible hypothesis, then, that at the beginning of his ministry Jesus neither acknowledged nor believed himself the Messiah. But his growing experience aroused the idea within him. Let me speak briefly of three factors of his experience which may have suggested the belief:

First, the ever present and urgent hopes of the multitude and of his disciples. John was asked—"Art thou the Messiah?" And, of course, the question was forced upon Jesus also. The ambitious Twelve, moreover, may very well have nursed this hope, so that both from the multitude and from those nearest Jesus, the idea was pressed upon him from without.

Secondly, the question was arising also from within, prompted especially by his power over demoniacs. It is unquestionable that Jesus actually possessed this power. We may deem it the power of a mighty personality over persons temporarily deranged, but Jesus did not so interpret it. In his eyes, it was power over evil spirits, and although

THE THEOLOGICAL METHOD OF JESUS

such power was not peculiar to himself, he may well have
possessed it to an extraordinary degree. But what did this
power over the hosts of evil mean? Jesus humbly inter-
preted it: "If I by the spirit of God cast out demons, then
is the Kingdom of God come upon you." (Matthew
12:28.) Doubtless, this was an exalted utterance in a
moment of deeply stirred feeling and may not represent,
at this time, a final conviction—but it shows the direction
in which his mind was moving. When the disciples of John
came with their master's inquiry, Jesus points them to the
wonders he was performing, leaving John to draw what
inference he would—almost as if he himself were not
wholly clear as to the possible meaning of this extraordinary supernatural power granted unto him.

A third influence was his own consciousness of peculiar nearness to God. That he knew God better than
the men about him he was sure—and was he not right?
But was this superior knowledge due to his own wit, or
was it that God had chosen him, and that from the Father
his word and works proceeded? This he undoubtedly believed. But if God had chosen him for a great purpose,
why was not God indicating him as the Messiah by the
words and works manifest through him?

In these three ways, not to speak of others such as the
stories of the demoniacs, the progressive experience of
Jesus favored the rise of the Messianic conviction within
him. Apparently, however, he is still unconvinced until
the stage of his experiences is reached just prior to Caesarea Philippi. Holding in general, apparently, the idea of
a Messiah of judgment and glory, such as John had

preached, he feels that his work is that of a prophet and teacher. But it becomes evident that to continue in that work will bring him unto persecution and death. He then feels himself peculiarly set apart by God to a work where persecution will result in suffering and death. At this point—so we may conjecture—the idea dawns that so also in the Scriptures the Messiah appears to be persecuted, as well as to be the glorious and triumphant deliverer. But both representations must be true. May it not be, then, that the Messiah has a twofold mission: that he comes first to teach and warn in a ministry terminated by death and then returns a second time in power and glory? When we read that directly after confessing himself the Messiah to his disciples he began to teach them that the Son of Man must suffer many things and finally be put to death, it looks as if this idea of the Messiah had been accepted by him, and thus, let me repeat, through his growing experiences he has come to believe himself the Messiah. The process of the growth of the idea may thus be traceable to his unfolding experience and correlated with it.

II. Jesus' Attitude Toward the Outside World

Jesus' attitude toward the Gentile world must be treated much more briefly. If, at the time previously referred to, he bids his disciples hold aloof from the Samaritans and the Gentiles, if he declares, "I am not sent save unto the lost sheep of the house of Israel," if in the coasts of Tyre and Sidon he says to the Syrophenician woman, "It is not meet to take the children's bread and to cast it unto the dogs,"—we must see in him still the narrow vision necessitated by his belief in the nearness of the Messiah's coming. Yet his experience had been that there had not been so great faith in Israel as in the centurion. He had been led to the expectation that many would come from the east and the west to sit down in the Messiah's Kingdom. His experience, however, does not apparently bring him to a final conviction until after he accepts the Messianic idea with the death it involved. He then began to raise the question as to the meaning of this suffering and death. He finds it, apparently, in the assurance that in some way not clearly formed, the blessings of the Kingdom of God were then to be open to the Gentiles as well as the Jews.

In these two particulars, therefore, we may perhaps see the thought of Jesus growing with his experience, shaped and determined by it.

But now we must turn to see how he dealt logically with this experience of his. Of course, we cannot find the method everywhere applied. We do not find it, for example, in the instances we have just been considering. It is by no means meant, when reference is made to his logical method, either that he invariably reasons according to it or that he ever consciously formulated it. But it is a method which appears so often in his thought and is so very significant withal, that it deserves special mention and consideration.

How then did Jesus deal with the materials which, as we have seen, were furnished by his experiences? Is it possible to detect any principle of logical inference by which from these materials his thought was ordered?

Of Hillel's seven rules, the first, which remained the first also in the rules of Rabbi Ishmael, was what was called the rule of Qal-ve-Chomer or Light and Heavy. The rule is very simple in character and operation, corresponding to our *a fortiori* method of argument. If, for example, a certain restriction holds in a case of comparatively slight importance, must it not hold good also in a case of great importance? If it is allowable to do a certain thing for an animal on a feast or holy day, surely it is allowable to do the same thing for a man. Evidently the rule is susceptible of an almost infinite variety of applications. And it is, plainly, a perfectly natural and obvious method of reasoning. We need not suppose, therefore, that Jesus was consciously borrowing a rabbinical method or even that he was consciously using a logical method at all, when we find him employing this *a fortiori* method of argument. The Rabbis applied it to the words of Scripture, Jesus to laws of nature and of human life.

In the ways of nature, Jesus observed that God clothed the lilies and fed the birds. His argument is plain. "If God so clothe the grass of the field which today is and tomorrow is cast into the oven, shall he not much more clothe you, O ye of little faith?" Why are ye anxious—if not a sparrow falleth to the ground without your Father—are not ye of much more value than they, and will not He who watches over the sparrow *a fortiori* watch over the man? A similar argument is applied to materials derived from the world of human life. How often a sentence begins—"What man of you?" The argument is: if man ought to deal thus with man, much more will God deal thus with man. "If ye, then, being evil, know how to give good gifts unto your children, how much more shall your Father who is in heaven give good things to them that ask him?" If a shepherd goeth after a sheep that is lost until he find it, how much more is a man than a sheep, how much more faithful is God than a human shepherd? Will not, then, God seek and find the wandering man who is His child? So, too, Jesus' nature and human life tell of God and yet how much more!

His method is found over and over again in the parables. If an unjust judge yields to the importunities of a persistent suitor, surely much more will God avenge His own elect who similarly call upon Him. If a friend will arise at last at the earnest desire of a friend to give him bread to set before a guest, will not God much more respond to the beseeching of His children? If a shepherd rejoices over a recovered sheep, a woman over a recovered coin, a father over a son who was lost but is found, is there not much more rejoicing in the presence of God over one sinner that repenteth? And if neighbor and friend do not refuse to share the joy of the shepherd, the woman, the father, ought not a Pharisee also much more to share in the rejoicing, when a son of God returns to his father's heart and home? "What man of you!" "How much more!" These are the words which ring repeatedly through the teachings of Jesus, as he rises from the ways of nature and of men to the ways of God.

This, then, is the principal logical method of Jesus. As God deals with man in nature, so He deals with the soul of man. If His minor gifts of sunshine and shower are be-

stowed impartially upon the evil and the good, the just
and the unjust, is not His mercy much more over the soul
of man? If man deal thus tenderly with man, surely God is
not less tender than man, and what man does or ought to
do for man, God will do for him. Plainly, this is but the
argument of Browning's Saul when David, looking com-
passionately upon the stricken king, reasons thus:

Do I find love so full in my nature, God's ultimate gift,
That I doubt his own love can compete with it?
    Here, the parts shift?
Here, the creature surpass the Creator,—the end, what Began?
Would I fain in my impotent yearning do all for this man,
And dare doubt he alone shall not help him, who yet alone can?

It will make Jesus' use of this principle clearer, if we
glance at it in its ethical aspect, for we may argue that as
man ought to deal with man, so God deals with him; or we
may argue that as God deals with man, so man ought to
deal with his brother. It is really the same principle, only
looked at now in its religious, now in its ethical aspect.
Jesus used it in both ways. For instance, God bestows His
kindness upon both good and evil—"He is kind unto the
unthankful and the evil," therefore do you who are children of God also love your enemies—"Ye therefore shall
be perfect even as your Father in heaven is perfect." In
the light of this principle, we understand some of the
most perplexing sayings of Jesus. He bids his followers
give to every one that asketh. But the reason for it is this:
"Ask and ye shall receive, seek and ye shall find, knock
and it shall be opened unto you." Treat men as God treats
you, that is the law. "Freely ye have received, freely give."

[66]

He counsels non-resistance. Why? Simply because God does not strike back. The evil man goes on his evil way and there comes no bolt from the sky in token of God's wrath. God does not strike back—"I say unto you, love your enemies, and pray for them that persecute you, that ye may be sons of your Father who is in heaven, for He maketh His sun to rise on the evil and the good and sendeth rain on the just and the unjust." God does not resist the evil man, therefore God's child must treat men as his Father treats them. From the point of view of the religious aspect, the ways of nature and of man as he ought to be are revelations of God's dealings with men. From the point of view of the ethical aspect, God deals with men as men at their best know they ought to deal with one another. Treat men as God treats them, that ye may be the sons of your Father who is in heaven. Herein lies the clue to the distinctive ethical and religious thought of Jesus. Not, let me repeat, that he had consciously and deliberately formulated such a rule as this. Yet it is exemplified in his teaching over and over again, and in accordance with it his mind worked. Looking at nature and at man, he reasoned "how much more." Hence from both nature and man came just, though insufficient, revelations of the nature and operations of God.

Observe, also, how this principle underlies his teaching when it rests upon his own inner experience. I have spoken of his experiences in the world of nature and of man first, in order to show that it was while he was so living, and not in the least in an ecstatic state, that the marvelous inner

[67]

experiences of communion with God were his. The point of prime importance, where one is dealing with this deepest experience of Jesus, is the sort of man in whom it is found. And the realism of Jesus is the best surety for his idealism. The normality of his experience when it lies within our ken inspires confidence in its equal normality when it goes beyond our vision into the secret place of the soul, where man and God come together. Jesus argued from the deepest feelings of his own soul by the same method up to God from whom they proceeded and of whom they bore witness.

He boldly spoke the word of forgiveness of sins, and men asked then, as they have often asked since—"Who can forgive sin save God alone?" But such a question ignores entirely Christ's method of thought. In his own heart of holiness, he found pity and forgiveness for this sinful man or woman; was his heart kinder than God's? Was his love for a wayward brother beyond God's love for an erring son? If, therefore, with all his deep hatred of sin, he found loving forgiveness for the penitent sinner, could he not be certain that God also forgave? So, quite in the spirit of the Hebrew prophets who were his spiritual predecessors, he ascribed his thought and feeling to God and in God's name spoke as God's prophet. And when he gave to his followers power to forgive sins, can we for an instant suppose that it was an official function which he was bestowing upon them? Assuming that his followers were living in his spirit, their feeling of forgiveness would have like value to his own, and from their own love they could venture to speak boldly in God's name of God's love. Similarly, he said of publicans and sinners that they went into the Kingdom of Heaven before the Pharisees, and of the publican who proclaimed himself the sinner, that he went down to his house justified rather than the Pharisee who also deemed himself one in a class for virtue as the publican deemed himself one for evil. When he thus spoke, what was the secret of his bold declaration? Was it that he was conscious of some unique authority thus to judge and to speak, or was it simply in harmony with the principle of which we are speaking that finding in himself greater love for penitent publican than for proud Pharisee, he felt sure that in this he was truly representative of God Himself? Nothing could be more natural and inspiring than such trustful boldness. It is a thousand pities that this personal authority should have been made, in Christian thinking, an official authority and thus restricted to Jesus alone, while his great method of thought has been forgotten and neglected.

How did he know that the distinction between clean and unclean meats was not of God, that all the petty restrictions of which others made so much were of no account before God? Was it not because he found that, living without reference to these things, his relations to God were unaffected? God did not forsake him when he sat with publicans and sinners at meat—therefore for such things God did not care. It was a human experience over against an *a priori* and conventional judgment. So Job erects his conscious innocence over against the traditional doctrine and will not give the lie to his own experience, though by affirming it he is led to deny a popular dogma

[69]

and even impugn the justice of God Himself. Let us compare small, modern things with things great and ancient. A century ago, there lived here in New England William Ellery Channing. Now, according to the theology of his time, this man could not live in God's grace because his creed denied what were supposed to be the intellectual conditions of communion with God. And yet he knew, himself to be, and as years went on, all men acknowledged that he was a man who lived with God. In the light of that fact, when its significance was fully apprehended, the insistence upon certain intellectual beliefs as essential to communion with God had to weaken. In the light of the great fact of the life, the creed vanished. So, in a far greater way, was it with Jesus. In his time, certain conditions were emphasized as conditions of communion with God—things which seem trivial enough to us today but which then bulked large because they were supposed to have been established and ordained by God Himself. Jesus paid no heed to these, and still he was conscious that to his pure heart, God was revealed, and that he did abide in conscious communion with God. This experience was decisive. Speaking, as always, out of his own experience, Jesus taught the simple essence of religion as love to God and love to man—the heart of the Law and the Prophets. Herein was the secret of Jesus' supreme power. His religious life was not a life of hearsay, but of personal experience, and upon that personal experience his word rested. God was in communion with him. This he knew, of this he was profoundly conscious. That communion was not destroyed. God's approval was thus given to his words and deeds which were no longer his, but God's. His love was God's love, but God's love far exceeded his. Thus he taught and thus he lived, with an authority personal, not derived, which has carried through the ages, and which today makes the experience of Jesus of Nazareth the supremely significant fact of human history. His thoughts live, because they were built on his own experience. He reasoned from his own experience in the world of nature and of men up to the reality of God.

There was one ruling idea in the mind of Jesus, the relation of which to his method was probably not discerned by his own mind, but which we shall have to emphasize when we discuss the validity of the method. Therefore I shall venture to speak upon it briefly. It is plain that the Kingdom of God had become one of the chief thought forms of his mind, with reference to which all questions and experiences were viewed. "Seek ye first the Kingdom of God," he taught. He sought it first himself, and it was a ruling idea. But what did he mean by the Kingdom of God? Within a generation, scholarly opinion has made a complete shift with regard to this matter. Earlier scholars, idealizing Jesus to such an extent that they shrank from ascribing to him any but the very loftiest ideas and totally unwilling to credit him with ideas that were erroneous, were almost unanimous in holding that the apocalyptic and eschatological ideas ascribed to him in the Gospels and supposed to be the staple of contemporary thought, were not really held by him. It was considered that they only represented the reflections of later disciples with their carnal expectations and grossly material views. Of late, however, the pendulum has completely swung back, and we are now told that the eschatological elements were really his and that teachings of an apparently different character have been misunderstood and actually are expressions of the crude and common notions.

It is not for us now to enter into this controversy. If I may in a few sentences suggest my own thought, I should say that the passages which appear to represent both views are to be taken at their face value, and that the belief, which has maintained itself in the Christian church as a whole from the beginning, more nearly represents the mind of Jesus than the opinions of the critics a generation ago or today. That is, the simplest and most natural idea is that Jesus believed in the Kingdom of God as both present and growing in the world and to be consummated in the near future by a catastrophic coming of the Kingdom of God in power and glory. His parables of nature seem to contain the clue to the way in which he united the two conceptions. The seed is cast into the ground, it germinates and grows until the time of the harvest which is a catastrophic event. Such is the Kingdom of God according to the view of Jesus. It was at that time present in the world, as witnessed particularly by the manifest power over evil spirits. "If I by the finger of God cast out devils, then is the Kingdom of God come upon you." This Kingdom, however, was to grow like the mustard plant and spread like the leaven, until the time of God's appointment when, by the reappearance of the Messiah, the Kingdom was to be actually established upon the earth.

[72]

That the disciples were not bidden to work for the Kingdom, that, in truth, no effort of theirs could hasten its
revelation which stood already in the determination of
the Father, is probably true. It is probably also true that
Jesus expected his own return as the Messiah of glory, and
the establishment of the Kingdom within the generation
of men then living. In these two particulars, as well as in
the notion of the catastrophic setting up of the Kingdom,
the thought of Jesus may have become meaningless to us.
But, whatever may be said on these points or in general
about his thought as to the way in which the Kingdom
was to be realized, there can be no doubt that he confidently believed that the time was coming in which men
should live together upon the earth as members of one
family in mutual love and trust, children of the one
Father. This he designated as the Kingdom of God. This
was but the old prophetic hope of a day in which the
law of God should be universally obeyed, and God Himself should be acknowledged as Lord through all the
earth. As might be expected, the attention of Jesus is
concentrated upon the ethical characteristics of this Kingdom, rather than upon its outward glory. Its citizens
are to be the childlike in spirit, not the proud and
arrogant, but the meek, the peacemakers, the pure in
heart, the poor in spirit. That is, the Kingdom of God
meant for him a state in which the ethical qualities were
to prevail everywhere in the world. These were the winning things in the world, they were to grow and spread
as the influence of his teaching extended. At God's own
appointed time He was to cast out and destroy all else, so

that these might survive alone. This was Jesus' great hope and expectation, and as such it was plainly one of the ruling ideas of his life with reference to which all other ideas were judged, and all values established. Now this hope of the Kingdom of God may seem to have very little, indeed, no affiliation with the *a fortiori* method which was constructive in his thought. Nevertheless, we shall see later, when we come to discuss the present validity of his theological method, that the two ideas really belong together, and that both must have place in the theological construction of today.

Let us then sum up the results so far obtained: Jesus' thought did not rest upon Scripture or traditions, but upon personal experience. That experience was not in ecstatic moments, but in the normal ways of nature and the ordinary paths of men. By a most simple, logical method he argued from the facts of his experience up to the will of God, with perfect belief in truth and good will as the supreme forces of the world, whose supremacy was to become visible in the Kingdom of God.

LECTURE VII.

THE VALIDITY OF JESUS' THEOLOGICAL METHOD

FINALLY, we have to inquire into the validity and present utility of the theological method of Jesus. The suggestion that theology must be based upon the facts of religious experience ought to be accepted without question, although unfortunately it cannot be, for it has not always been held true. But if any science lays claim to be considered as a science at all, it must be because it is presented as an attempt to bring order into a group of facts. Hence if theology is a science, it should be a systematization of facts. But what are the facts? Are they the facts of Hebrew history, of the life of Christ or the words of the apostles—or are the facts of religion, experiences including, as will be shown hereafter, the religious experience of Israel, of Christ and his followers? This is crucial in theology, but the science of facts in the world of space and time is history, not theology, and theology ought to be the science of religious experiences. Too often theology has gone astray because it has not held fast to these known facts, but its zeal for systematizing has gone its way, regardless of the actuality of man's experience. When, therefore, we find Jesus dealing with the facts of his own religious experience, we realize that to this extent, at least, he is making use of a method which is valid and acceptable, indeed the only just method of theological study.

When, however, it is said that theology must be the systematizing of religious experience, we are instantly confronted by two objections which appear fatal to further progress. In reality, however, they open the way to large advance. The first is that a pure experience is for us entirely impossible. In truth, for an experience to become known as an experience, it must already have been affected by memory and to some degree, at least, correlated with other facts of mental life. Only the very lowest orders of life can have anything approximating a pure experience. But in this case there is probably a succession of discrete, unrelated feelings which cannot be known as experience. For us memory and correlation, with some sort of interpretation, are inextricably involved in each moment of present experience. Secondly, if theology rests upon individual experience, must not theology itself be wholly individual? My theology, that is, must be the interpretation of my experience, but my experience is mine and not another's. Hence how can my interpretation of it appeal to another? Thus, truth as we conceive truth would disappear from theology, and individualism alone would obtain. Doubtless the experience of Jesus needed such check and correction. We feel assured that in many respects this was done, but where are we to find such criteria? How can we be sure that his experience is normal and not merely personal, or pathological? Thus theology as the science of religious experience, at least of our experience, seems discredited at the outset.

It should be observed that precisely the same objections as those just mentioned are valid against all science whatsoever. No pure experience is possible anywhere. In every act of perception there is memory, correlation, and interpretation. There are certain mental forms, forms of perception, categories of the understanding, which modify every act of perception, so that a pure, unmixed perception or experience is nowhere possible. Kant has shown us this once and for all. Whether or not we hold these forms to be independent of all experience, or the ingrained results of long-continued racial experience, whether or not we deem them wholly erroneous so that all knowledge must be false just because it is a construction, or true because it represents the experience of the race and manifestly offers safe guidance, the fact remains that in all science and not in theology alone, a pure experience is for us wholly impossible. The underlying charges against theology as the science of experience hold equally against all science in strict logic. How can any one really know anything beyond his own perceptions? These alone we know, and we can pass beyond them to assumed realities in the sense-world or to other beings like ourselves only by an inference which so far, at least, we are absolutely powerless to validate. Theoretically, the difficulties are insurmountable. By strictly logical processes we find ourselves driven into solipsism. Then we set about trying to convince others of its truth, that our ideas are not ours alone, but have reality beyond our minds, and that there are others who can be, and ought to be, convinced of its truth. But here, as often, our native good sense gets the better of our vigorous philosophizings. It is plain, then, that theology, so far as these objections go, is in as bad case as all science.

How then, practically, do we get beyond this strict individualism to which strict philosophy theoretically condemns us? Let us consider first the individualism. Do we not overcome this by social intercourse, with its certain testing of experience, and by habitual dealing with what we assume to be the world of nature, which passes merciless judgment on our experiences and theories? We mingle with our fellows, converse with them, compare our experiences with theirs, and come to a sort of rude social agreement as to normality of experience, based upon its practically universal character. If, for instance, we see on the field a moving figure, but on indicating to friends standing by our side the spot where it appears we find that they see nothing corresponding to our vision, we unhesitatingly declare ourselves victims of an hallucination. Our perception is somehow awry. Or, again, if believing that a certain object is in a certain place, because we seem to see it there, we act as if it were really there and discover that the result of our action is not what we should expect it to be, if things were as they seem, we again conclude that our perception was erroneous and our experience abnormal. In a word, we recognize theoretically the difficulties of experience as the basis of all sciences. But practically we overcome them by habitual intercourse with the world of nature and of man. No man, we say, who lives freely with his kind and is in constant touch with the world of concrete realities, is likely to be permanently or harmfully deluded as to the nature of his experience. But the experience of Jesus was the experience of one who, as we have seen, did thus know and live in intimate relations with the world of nature and the world of man. In this respect, again, his theological method was sound and valid.

Plainly, moreover, in particular realms one who is busy in scientific pursuits must test his experiences by those of men who are engaged in similar pursuits. There are general common experiences, but there are also particular experiences possible only for those who are especially interested in them and who put themselves in the way of receiving them. For instance, a botanist keeps his mind sane, in general, by intercourse with men and mingling in the common human life. But there are observations peculiar to his study which can be tested and confirmed or contradicted only by his associates in botanical study, who undertake similar experiments and report their several experiences. Similarly, with regard to religious experience, a man must not only have general sanity, that is normality of mind, but he must compare his experience with those of other religious men. In this way only is he particularly delivered from the danger of peculiarity and abnormality. Now in the case of Jesus, this was effected in two ways. In the first place, as we have seen, he was devoted to the Scriptures, especially to the prophetic portions. But, as we intimated in the first lecture, the prophets were men speaking out of a personal religious experience. We have to thank the science of the Higher Criticism for presenting the Bible to us in this light. It provides intercourse with the great prophets of Israel and other souls who have sought and found genuine religious experience. Furthermore, Jesus did not claim uniqueness for his experience, but called his disciples to follow him. It is just because through all the ages men who have taken Jesus seriously and sought to live in the way he taught, have had religious experiences like his, that we acknowledge his supreme authority in religion—an authority which grows as each new soul adopts his path of life and finds, as he found, the living presence of God. Thus, by his use of the Scripture and his calling upon men to follow him, the method of Jesus again commends itself as sound and valid. For us familiarity with the Bible and communion with the Church, in which we find other souls also seeking the experience of religion, serve the same end. For this purpose, the Bible is open to us as it was not to our forefathers, since it is now seen clearly to be a book of religious experience.

But alas! the great service of the church in finding the living presence of God is still to be rendered. Our divided Christendom tends to give to each denomination a particular type of religious experience, and a particularized theology based upon it. Associating only with those of his own fellowship, a man naturally tends to restrict his experience still more closely to the prevailing type, and to forget or ignore the existence of other types. Hence, we have denominational theologies. But a Christian theology must be the outcome at last of a Christian experience of a united church, to which each makes his individual contribution and in which there is a sifting of truths by the ultimate consensus of Christian souls. The Church of the past also gives its aid, if beneath the various formulas of faith and modes of expression we become able to discern the experience which they enshrine. This opens a field too large for our present inquiry, inviting though it is, and we must not pursue the thought further. It is enough now to have seen that by resort to experience in the world of nature and of man, Jesus was in the true path of theological thought, and that by his use of the Scripture and appeal to the experience of others adopting his way of life, he suggests the helpful use in theology of the Bible and the Church.

In what has been already said lies the justification of his use of the *a fortiori* method. The implication of that principle is the belief that in the processes of nature and of history we find revelations of God. The truth of this has become almost an axiom with us. Our theistic view of the world can but regard it as a manifestation of the one divine life. The laws of nature are revelations of the divine will. The course of human history is the disclosure of divine purpose, and in man as the child of God we see the crowning revelation of the nature of God. If from Him all things proceed, then the highest appearance must give us the truest idea of the real nature of the all productive Life. Certainly we may conclude that no exhibition of human love can transcend the nature out of which it has flowed. The love in man cannot surpass the love of God. Thus the argument of Jesus has irresistible force. "What man of you?" he asks. If man deals thus with man, will not God deal as gently and truly? Nay, our ideals are born of the same divine life, and our highest ideals of the relations between man and man are intimations of God's dealing with man. Thus for us the function of Jesus in theology is the achieved embodiment of our best ideal.

His experience is the experience of the highest type of human life. Never, therefore, can we, agreeing with the method of Jesus, think of God as showing less love and justice than prevails among men. Since we are growing men, growing in humane qualities, the ideals of men are ennobled, ever keeping in advance of the actual and established realities. But over our nobler ideals, the great words of Jesus shine—"how much more." "Father" is a nobler, purer word than it was a millenium or even a century ago. Its meaning deepens with the progress of man. The thought of the Heavenly Father gains correspondingly in beauty. But this is still the application of the method of Jesus Christ, and over the more glorious earthly fatherhood we hear his words—"If ye then, being evil, know how to give good gifts unto your children, how much more shall your Heavenly Father give good things to them that ask Him." In its use of the *a fortiori* method, therefore, as well as in its appeal to experience in the world of nature and of man, the method of Jesus is valid.

Just at this point, therefore, we meet the objection previously raised which we must not seek to evade by some trick word or phrase. If nature is to be viewed as the revelation of God, what sort of God is it whom it reveals? Jesus spoke happily and confidently of God who cares for the fall of a sparrow. Yet, as has been said, the sparrow falls, and through cruel hours beats its little life away in a vain struggle for existence. Does God feed the fowls of the air? They might have scant picking did not some of the sower's casting fall upon the beaten ground. Yet only a short time ago in neighboring towns notices were posted, urging citizens to make provision for birds in the Middlesex Fells, which were dying of hunger through the cold and dreary winter. And, as the doctrine of evolution by survival of the fittest has taught us, strife and suffering are not incidental in nature, but are wrought into the very fabric of things. John Stuart Mill has given us the scathing arraignment of nature, repeated with no less fervor by John Fiske, and set forth with merciless truth by Huxley in his famous *Romanes Lecture,* which asserted that man is not to copy nature, but is to set himself against its laws and processes. The observation of Jesus was superficial and since it was superficial, was not true. Our deeper view of nature gives us no such happy picture of the ways of God in nature as delighted his vision. Before this awful fact of suffering in the world, which we know more deeply than he could have known it, does not his sunny faith become almost ghastly? If God cares for the birds, how much more for man? But if his actual care for the mute creation is such as we now conceive it to be, what is the outlook for man? The argument of Jesus seems to fail dismally.

What about the ways of man? I referred above to Browning's Saul, which presents the argument of Jesus in lyric beauty. Even as I read, I wondered that some did not sarcastically interrupt me by saying, "What about Browning's Caliban?" The monster on his island watched the crabs crawling by and let a few go. Then he pinched the claws of another, out of sheer wanton cruelty, and argued precisely after the fashion of David. So Setebos. What

[83]

becomes of natural theology on the island when Caliban
is writing the argument? And there are Calibans in the
world. Here is the world of human life, all of which, together with the natural world, must be the product of the
same immanent God. How, in the presence of all this
tangled web of good and evil, joy and pain, can one reason
to such a God, the God in whom Jesus believed? In a
word, by what right do we select the good, ignoring the
evil, and then from that reason up to God, since, according
to our thought of the immanent God, all alike must have
proceeded from Him? Thus our theistic view of the
world, which makes it the expression of an immanent
God and which seemed to support the method of Jesus,
appears to involve us in inextricable difficulties.

> I falter where He firmly trod,
> And falling with my weight of cares
> Upon the world's great altar stairs,
> Which slope through darkness up to God,
> I stretch lame hands of faith and grope.

Altar stairs stained with the blood of innumerable victims, animal and human! We ask what value the argument
of Jesus has in relation to the world as we actually know it?

Yes, there is the difficulty. But let me remind you that
it besets not alone our thought of the immanent God, and
the argument of Jesus which ultimately rests upon it. It
besets every view of the world which brings God into any
sort of causal relation to it, and any theistic argument
which seeks to ground itself where every valid argument

[84]

must ultimately ground itself: in the actual fact of exis-tence. After all, is not the Setebos of Caliban truer to the facts than the God of David or of Christ?

You will not expect me to give a satisfactory answer to this objection—nobody can do so, and I shall not pretend to. But there are suggestions helpful to me, which I may at least venture to repeat. It is the doctrine of evolution which has deepened our difficulties at this point. But let us not forget that from the same doctrine we derive the notion of a world in process. Is the world still in process? God made the world in six days—how strange that sounds in our ears, not because the time is so short but because of the assumption that the world is made, is done, a com-pleted product! If the world is still in process, then, as con-cerns it, the facts are not yet all collected. Where is the judge so unscrupulous as to pass sentence before all the evidence has been presented? Again, evolution has taught us to place man in the development of the world. But he is part of nature, man with his humanity, his love and hope, his gentleness and good will, the very highest we know of humanity. This, too, belongs in nature, and out of it he has come. Out of it, out of the cruelty has come, by nat-ural process, kindness; out of hate, love. Out of all this hideous welter, it seems to us, of suffering and strife have emerged, not in spite of it, but because of it, "the Lord Christ's heart, and Shakespere's brain." We must not be guilty of the fallacy of conceiving of this natural process as a cone with man at its apex, in whom all lines converge. This much is certain—that out of this world goodness has emerged and the human forces are actually proving themselves the winning forces in the world. With this in mind, certain that David is to displace Caliban and that man has actually shown himself capable of transforming nature into godliness and beauty, must we not hesitate before allowing this objection to sweep us off our feet? Nay, may we not go farther than this and say that from what we know of the world, it appears to justify the faith of Jesus in the ultimate appearance of the Kingdom of God? Here we discover the relation between his hope and method—his method would be of comparatively little service to us, were it not for his hope. If we may, however, conceive of this world as in process towards the Kingdom of God, then, although difficulties naturally enough remain, since we are dealing with an unfinished process, at best but very imperfectly known, we may say that the world has cared for the things for which God cared by producing, maintaining, and increasing them. We shall still find in the proc esses of nature and of man and in the growth of holy lives, the Kingdom of God, the revelation of God. Ah, you reply, but that is at best only a splendid hope and faith. Yes, but it is a hope and a faith which is by no means without probable validity in the world as we know it. Let us, however, accept this hope for the present merely as a hope, reserving for faint credulity the doubt just suggested and for the present affirming this hope as an expression of our theistic faith.

Our theistic view of the world affirms that not only is this a world of process, but it is also a world of progress; it is a growing world. It is growing toward an end worthy of Him of whose nature the unfolding process is progressive manifestation. How shall we phrase our conception of the end toward which the whole creation moves better than by saying that the world is in process toward the Kingdom of God? If it be really as we believe—that the inmost law of the world is the good will of the Eternal One—is it not certain that as by experience in the world man inevitably learns to know and obey its laws—for only thus is he able to survive in the world at all—so he must come ultimately to know and obey the law of good will? If it be true that we are all members one of another, man must ultimately acknowledge that fact and live in harmony with it. The theistic view of the world, then, means that the world is on its way to the sort of human society which Jesus had in mind when he looked forward to the Kingdom of God. It is true—let us remind ourselves of this once more—it is true that the precise form in which Jesus conceived of this Kingdom cannot be ours, any more than we can hold to his view of the way in which the Kingdom was to be realized. But his hope, the hope of Israel, of a coming order in which men should live together in mutual trust and love as members of the one family of God, that hope is ours.

If we indulge this hope, it behooves us to take it very seriously and make it a ruling, constructive idea in our theological thinking. Science has taught us that nothing can be rightly understood, save genetically. This particular event or institution, for instance, has a history, and only by knowing how it came to be can we properly understand it as it now is. All things, therefore, being in process are to be studied with reference to the process.

This is the historical method which governs our study today. But if all things are thus in process, is the process now complete? Surely the end has not yet been reached. If we can understand the present only by reference to the past, can we understand the past save by reference to the present? But if the process still continues, and the present has already, while we are considering it, become the past, then must we not say that no present event or institution can be rightly understood and judged, save with reference to the future? All things are truly known only as they are truly seen in the process of the world toward the Kingdom of God. That is the principle which results from taking seriously the scientific teaching as to the world process, and the religious faith as to the world progress. Hence the idea of the Kingdom of God must become a governing idea in our theological thought. In the light of this firm idea, the method of Jesus seems to be valid and of present applicability.

In the case of every real and fruitful thinker, the method of his thinking is usually of more importance than the results obtained, because when the method is once grasped and accepted, it can be applied to facts and problems which had not come within his ken. But has the church been true to the method of its Master, with all the honor it has paid to his specific teaching? Has its theology been based upon human experience? Think, for instance, of the treatment of sin in Christian theology, how unreal and fantastic it has usually been, how utterly untrue to the facts of human experience! Has it honored the ways of nature and of men? How many systems of theology have

been constructed by men with no eye for nature and no
real sympathetic fellowship with humanity? Nay, sometimes by men who have deliberately held aloof, deeming
all nature and men—save the regenerate alone—under
the curse and virtually given over to evil, so that the natural human sentiments have been explicitly denied a right
to be heard in questions of theology. Has it adopted the
method of "how much more." How often has the God of
systematic theology been baser than the man of popular
approval and credited with conduct which would be repro-
bated in man! Has it held to the faith in the Kingdom of
God? Have its theories of punishment and forgiveness
been constructed with an eye single to the restoration of
the man who had sinned and to the ways of the spirit that
moves toward the Kingdom of God? Shall we not, as
Christians, return to the method of Jesus, redeeming theology from its often deserved name of the dismal science,
making it fresh, vital, progressive, Christian? There is a
deal of foolish talk to the effect that men are weary of
theology. They are weary of untrue and unreal theology.
But never was there a greater need and craving than now
for a true theology, for a theology which follows the
method of Jesus. Let us not be blind to the fact that there
are immense difficulties in the way of such a method.
There are terrible problems which as yet we cannot solve,
but I am convinced that their solution is possible. It is
possible, however, only by the untrammeled use of the
simple method of experience in the ways of nature and of
man, from which we reason to God manifest, but not ex-

[89]

hausted by all, and governed by faith in the progress of this world toward the Kingdom of God.

All this, it may be said, however, proceeds upon the theistic view of the world which to many men is the point of deepest uncertainty. Does not this method presuppose the very thing about which our doubt is deepest? Yes, that is a valid objection to the method as stated so far. But let us accept the doubt and deny that for us the theistic view of the world is established. Nevertheless, we know that we ought to work for the coming of a social order in which all men shall be governed by the family feeling, for a social state in which justice prevails and good will governs. Whether there be a God or not, whether the theistic view of the world be true or not, every true heart answers to the call and the challenge of this ideal, which is precisely the ideal which we have denominated the Kingdom of God. But if for this ideal we ought to work and to it we should dedicate our lives, it must be the governing idea in our thought, shaping our plans, governing our purposes and ambitions. How can we realize this ideal, save by learning the laws of the world and the ways of man, that is, by experience with nature and with men by which alone we can help toward the realization of our ideal? And most of all by honoring our ideals, if not by declaring them at present real in the purpose of God, then at least by declaring them real in our purpose and giving prompt and loyal obedience to every greatening purpose. The point is this, that whether the theistic view of the world be true or not, every man ought to live as if it were true, giving his life to the ideal which it presents and encourages. Thus and only thus, as I firmly believe, one comes to believe profoundly in the theistic view of the world. To live the life of Jesus is the way to make ours the faith and hope of Jesus. To live by the method of Jesus is to come to full personal conviction, through an experience which is for us finally authoritative, that the God in whom he believed and trusted is our God; that we are in very truth His children, living and working in His growing world, and that our determinations are His purposes, our ideals are disclosures of His will, our hopes His promises, our aspirations, His aspirations.